4/19

THE WHITE HOUSE

BY BARBARA

Gareth Stevens
PUBLISHING

Please visit our website, www.garethstevens.com. For a free color catalog of all our high-quality books, call toll free 1-800-542-2595 or fax 1-877-542-2596.

Cataloging-in-Publication Data

Names: Linde, Barbara M.
Title: The White House / Barbara M. Linde.
Description: New York : Gareth Stevens Publishing, 2019. | Series: Symbols of America | Includes glossary and index.
Identifiers: ISBN 9781538232323 (pbk.) | ISBN 9781538229019 (library bound) | ISBN 9781538232330 (6 pack)
Subjects: LCSH: White House (Washington, D.C.)–Juvenile literature. | Washington (D.C.)–Buildings, structures, etc.–Juvenile literature.
Classification: LCC F204.W5 L56 2019 | DDC 975.3–dc23

Published in 2019 by
Gareth Stevens Publishing
111 East 14th Street, Suite 349
New York, NY 10003

Designer: Sarah Liddell
Editor: Joshua Turner

Photo credits: Cover, p. 1 Rob Crandall/Shutterstock.com; p. 5 AgnosticPreachersKid/Wikimedia Commons; p. 7 Charles Phelps Cushing/ClassicStock/Archive Photos/Getty Images; pp. 9, 11 photo courtesy of Library of Congress; p. 13 O'Dea/Wikimedia Commons; p. 15 The Washington Post/Contributor/The Washington Post/Getty Images; p. 17 (blue and green rooms) Barry Winiker/Photolibrary/Getty Images; p. 17 (red room) TIM SLOAN/Staff/AFP/Getty Images; p. 19 glenda/Shutterstock.com; p. 21 George Rose/Contributor/Getty Images News/Getty Images.

Printed in the United States of America

CPSIA compliance information: Batch #CW19GS: For further information contact Gareth Stevens, New York, New York at 1-800-542-2595.

CONTENTS

Boldface words appear in the glossary.

A Famous Address

One of the most well-known addresses in the world is 1600 Pennsylvania Avenue in Washington, DC. It's the White House, the home of the US president and his family. The White House is a **symbol** of our country and its **democracy**.

Building the White House

George Washington thought the president should have a large, fancy house. Nine **architects** sent in their ideas. Washington picked one he liked, and the house was built between 1792 and 1801. It has always been painted white.

Moving In

Washington left office before the White House was finished, so he never lived in it. John Adams, the second president, was the first president to live in the White House. All other presidents have lived in it with their families.

9

Making Changes

President Benjamin Harrison put electricity in the White House in 1891. President Theodore Roosevelt built the West Wing in 1902. President Franklin Roosevelt made more changes starting in 1933. The East Wing as it stands today was finished in 1942.

WEST WING, 1934

11

The White House Today

The White House has 132 rooms, 35 bathrooms, 8 staircases, and 3 elevators. There are bowling alleys, a gym, and a library. The movie theater has enough seats for about 50 people. A court for tennis and basketball, swimming pool, and track are outside.

WHITE HOUSE MOVIE THEATER

13

The West Wing

The president and his **staff** work in the West Wing. The president works in the Oval Office. The **Cabinet** meets in the Cabinet Room. Important talks take place in the Situation Room. Members of the **press** also have rooms where they can work.

OVAL OFFICE

The Executive Residence

The president and the First Family live on the second floor of the central building of the White House. The Blue, Green, Red, and Yellow Rooms are on the first floor. The president greets world leaders and other guests here. The largest room, the East Room, is used for dances, parties, and meetings.

RED ROOM

BLUE ROOM

GREEN ROOM

17

The East Wing

The First Lady and her staff have offices in the East Wing. The social secretary's office plans all of the events for the White House. Another East Wing office prints cards, letters, and other papers. Tours of the White House start in the East Wing, too.

EAST WING HALLWAY

Visit the White House

A tour of the White House is free, but you need a ticket. You have to ask your member of **Congress** a few weeks before you go for tickets. There are hundreds of years of American history to see inside the White House!

GLOSSARY

architect: a person who plans buildings

Cabinet: a group of government leaders who give advice to the president

Congress: the group of government leaders who have been chosen by the citizens to make the laws for the country

democracy: the free and equal right of every person to participate in a government

press: television, radio, newspaper, and magazine workers

staff: the people who work for a person, the government, or a business

symbol: a picture, shape, or object that stands for something else

FOR MORE INFORMATION

BOOKS

Flynn, Sarah Wassner. *1,000 Facts About the White House.* Des Moines, IA: National Geographic Books, 2017.

Sabuda, Robert. *The White House: A Pop-Up of Our Nation's Home.* London, England: Orchard Books, Pop Edition, 2015.

WEBSITES

American History for Kids: Fun Facts About the White House
www.americanhistoryforkids.com/the-white-house/
Read interesting, unusual facts about the White House.

White House for Kids
clintonwhitehouse4.archives.gov/WH/kids/html/home.html

This site is designed to give young children and students fun facts about the history of the White House.

INDEX